Prehistoric Indians of Wisconsin

•

by
Robert E. Ritzenthaler

Revised
by
Lynne G. Goldstein

Third edition, 1985

•

Milwaukee Public Museum

Library of Congress Cataloging-in-Publication Data

Ritzenthaler, Robert Eugene, 1911-
   Prehistoric Indians of Wisconsin.

   Bibliography: p.
   1. Indians of North America — Wisconsin — Antiquities.
2. Wisconsin — Antiquities.   I. Goldstein, Lynne.
II. Title.
E78.W8R5   1985   977.5'1   85-15532
ISBN 0-89326-114-9

Design   Gregory Raab
Production Supervisor   Mary Garity
Photography   Mel Scherbarth
Photocomposition   Kenneth D. Lefevre, Parnau Graphics
Printing   The Fox Company
Specimen Coordination   Tom Kehoe, Claudia Jacobson

*Cover: The Miller Great Owl Effigy Pipe
made of Ohio pipestone. It was found by
Towne L. Miller in 1933 in Green Lake
County, Wisconsin.*

*Back cover: Characteristic Middle
Mississippi projectile points.*

Contents

Introduction

This book is a revised version of *The Prehistoric Indians of Wisconsin,* written in 1953 by Dr. Robert E. Ritzenthaler, then Curator of Anthropology at the Milwaukee Public Museum. Most of the illustrations in this edition of the book are the same as those in the 1953 version — the difference is in the interpretation of the illustrations and facts. Archaeology has changed considerably in the last thirty years, and this update presents recent findings and interpretations. As Ritzenthaler himself noted:

"The picture of the life of these peoples will not be complete because we do not know the whole story. What we do know is the result of work primarily by archaeologists, the men and women who delve into the past by excavating the remains of a people left in the earth, or by studying the evidences still to be found on the surface.

"The story will always be incomplete because the only evidence the archaeologist has to work with is in the form of material things which have either been accidentally preserved or are of such durable substance as to have withstood the destructive forces of nature."

While it is true that archaeologists only find a portion of the total picture, the developments of new methods and techniques allow us to gather new information and to look at old information in new ways. While there will be some things that archaeologists can probably never know, we have learned many things which we never thought could be learned thirty years ago.

Archaeologists try to determine how prehistoric people lived and how they

1

used the land around them. To do this, the artifacts and garbage left behind are examined, as well as the locations in which these items were found. A location where evidence of past human activity is found is called an *archaeological site.*

When you mention the word archaeology to most people, they think of King Tut, ancient Greece or Rome, or the pyramids of Mesoamerica. To many of us, archaeology is romantic — piecing together clues of the past, and finding fabulous riches of lost civilizations. TV and movies have, of course, helped us develop these images of archaeology — from the daring adventurer to the curse of the mummy's tomb.

Archaeology is more complex than this, and usually less romantic. Archaeologists use shovels, trowels, brushes and whisk brooms, but also need other tools such as radiocarbon dating, X-ray diffraction, neutron activation, soil profiles, aerial photographs, and computers. Likewise, archaeologists often call upon other specialists, such as geologists, botanists, and zoologists. Only a small portion of time is spent digging — most of the time archaeologists sit in a laboratory, carefully examining small bits and pieces of evidence, as well as photographs, maps, and soil samples. While archaeologists thirty years ago spent their time on *some* of these same tasks, we have learned a lot from their work and have developed new techniques and procedures.

The three goals of archaeology today include: 1) the construction of cultural chronologies or "timelines"; 2) the reconstruction of past lifeways; and 3) the search for the processes of culture

change. When the first version of this booklet was written, archaeologists were still working on the first goal, and were making good progress on the second. While we have not completed or abandoned the first two goals today, we have focused on learning more detail, and are beginning to work on the third goal.

Archaeologists can examine long and unbroken sequences of cultures. Only archaeologists can study the cultures of those who lived before writing, and that includes about ninety-eight percent of human history. Unfortunately, figuring out the specific details of when something happened is often tricky, and this is the purpose of the first goal — *chronology* — the ordering by time. We have to know when and in what order before we can consider how, who, what, or why.

Secondly, we want to know what these past societies were like — how did they live, where did they live, what did they eat, and how was their society organized. The answers to these questions mean that we have to do more than dig a single site — often, such work requires many years of research in an entire geographic region, because people moved around a lot and we need to understand all parts of their life and how they interacted with their specific environment.

The third goal is the most difficult to explain and to do. Archaeologists want to do more than observe, describe, and integrate — they want to *explain* the past. Thirty years ago, reports often focused on the artifacts and other material remains which were found, without a lot of discussion or analysis of the society which created those remains. The people behind the artifacts were sometimes forgotten. Today, we try to understand and learn more about the past and its relationship to the present.

People often think that prehistoric people lived a hard life, and that our present way of life is better than anything else could be. But when we consider other people in other places at other times, we have to maintain a perspective of *cultural relativism.* We must view other societies on their terms, not ours. Our way is not the only way to do things. In fact, in some situations our way might not work out so well. Prehistoric people were much more vulnerable to changes in their environment than we like to think we are, and to survive in the long run, they had to maintain a balance with nature. They were much better at maintaining this balance than we have been, and we can learn a lot by looking to the ways of the past.

Prehistoric Wisconsin was a land of plenty. There were many different plants and animals to choose as food, such as various kinds of fish and shellfish, turtles, deer, rabbits, muskrats and other small mammals, as well as nuts, grasses, and berries. It is unlikely that our forebears led a constant quest for food — they probably had to work no more than a few hours per day to get the materials they needed. While a two or three hour work day sounds marvelous, we shouldn't go to the other extreme and think of prehistoric people leading a romantic, idyllic lifestyle. There were dangers, disappointments, and disease, but there is also clear evidence of people caring about and for each other — for example, they maintained the old and sick even though these people could no longer participate in the gathering of food.

Excavating at an archaeological site in Jefferson County. Trowels and other small hand tools are used to even out the floor and to ensure that artifacts and features are discovered.

Hillock garden beds on the Carroll College campus, Waukesha.

Archaeological Methods
and Techniques

Finding Sites

The most common question that people ask archaeologists is "how do you know where to look?" or "how do you know where to dig?" Mounds, pyramids, crumbled walls of ancient cities or the pueblos of the Southwestern U.S. are easy to spot. But how does one decide that a cornfield or section of woods has an archaeological site worthy of investigation?

In order to locate sites, archaeologists conduct what is called a survey. There are two parts to a survey: one part has to do with *where* you look, and the other part concerns *how* you look. Traditionally, "where you look" has meant searching for archaeological sites in what people thought were likely places: spots like ridges or high ground along rivers and streams and lake shores. Not surprisingly, we find many sites in spots like these, and some people think that this was the only kind of location used by prehistoric people. But, if we look in *only* one kind of spot, is it really surprising that all of the sites are located there?

Archaeologists today try to understand *all* aspects of prehistoric societies. People's lives revolved around more than just one spot; they may have had a base camp, a series of hunting camps, fishing stations, and so on. People often moved to different locations at different times of the year. Not all of these different kinds of sites will yield splendid artifacts, but together they provide a much clearer picture of prehistoric people's lives. Try to think of yourself — how much would we really know about your entire life if we only examined *one* part — your house *or* your place of work *or* your school *or* where you buy food.

Today's archaeologists try to take a *regional* approach. An archaeologist will often work within an entire region — for example, a portion of a major river valley and its associated uplands — to try and determine all the kinds of sites present. We look for any and all traces of past human activities because people moved within regions seasonally to exploit the various potential sources of food and other necessities. By examining a large area, one is more likely to find the range of sites that were present and the kinds of resources exploited.

When an archaeologist examines a region, he or she wants to know where people lived, but also where they did *not* live. An understanding of both is necessary to reconstruct prehistoric lifeways. Usually, the archaeologist divides the region to be studied into small sections of land (maybe 40-acre units), then randomly chooses a percentage or proportion of these units to get a fair sample of all the different ecological and physical zones. While we all like to find artifacts, we often look as hard for nothing as for something. As one archaeologist noted, "It's not what you find that's important, it's what you find out."

While it is true that a small chip of stone will never be as exciting a find as a gold headdress or a whole pot, we now know that we can learn a lot from these bits and pieces of garbage left behind by prehistoric people. Archaeologists study the patterns of these items, as well as the items themselves, and from this evidence are able to determine much about the people who lived in prehistoric Wisconsin.

Context helps us to understand the past. Context implies not just where things were found, but also where they were found in relation to each other and other items around these items. Patterns of broken bits of bone may indicate that butchering of a deer took place on that site, and closer examination of the individual bones may tell us how the animal was killed and cleaned and eaten. We might even be able to tell how old the animal was when it died and in what season of the year it was killed. Likewise, small chips of stone may indicate how a beautiful spear pont was made, and its context may suggest how it was used. The questions asked, and even answered, become infinite with more small pieces of evidence collected. Long-distance trade, social organization, diet, technology, and many other things come within our grasp. Whole artifacts are relatively rare, but garbage is plentiful. Looking at *both* helps determine what people were doing and why they were doing it. The whole artifacts and impressive mounds and structures have much more meaning in their total context.

How we go about looking, once we have decided where to look, is relatively simple. In Wisconsin, two primary techniques are used to find sites — pedestrian survey and shovel probing. Pedestrian survey means systematically walking plowed land looking for evidence of prehistoric occupation. When a farmer plows the fields, the earth is churned up and any prehistoric site which is beneath ground surface may be disturbed. Rain and winds help expose these bits and pieces of rock and pottery and bone, and someone can be easily trained to spot such items. Archaeologists collect these items and plot their distribution and density — the technique can provide an estimate of how large the site is, how dense, what kinds of materials are present, and whether there seem to be concentrations of artifacts or activities. Most archaeological sites are found by pedestrian survey.

The other sort of survey technique is called shovel probing. This technique is used in areas where ground visibility is poor; this includes pastures, fallow fields, lawns, woodlots and forests. Surveyors space themselves at some predetermined interval (e.g., 10 or 15 meters), and at every interval along that swath dig a hole in the ground. The soil from that hole is carefully sifted for artifacts or other debris, and the soil textures and colors within the hole are also examined. Once the shovel probe hole is examined, it is immediately filled in, and the person proceeds to the next hole. When completed, the investigator has dug a patterned "grid" of holes across an area, and can determine whether or not a site is present. However, since only small holes are excavated at set intervals, the technique does not result in large quantities of artifacts or debris, and one cannot necessarily say much about the density or quantity of materials on a site. Also, if a site is very sparse or very small, it is possible that shovel probing will completely miss the site.

It is always possible that an archaeological survey will not result in the discovery of a site, even if a site is present. With shovel probing techniques, the difficulty comes from a site which is very sparse or small; from pedestrian survey, the difficulty may be collecting conditions (for example, whether or not it has rained recently), plowing practices, and the simple fact

Looking for sites: Pedestrian or walkover survey of plowed fields.

Pedestrian survey of a plowed field at equal intervals to ensure coverage. Flags are used to mark find spots.

that the site is buried deeper than the farmer plowed. Because of these difficulties, archaeologists try to survey areas more than one time if possible, and they also try to integrate information from other knowledgeable individuals.

The citizens of Wisconsin, especially farmers, are often the initial source of information about prehistoric sites. Farmers, who are very familiar with the details of their land, will often note mounds or unusual formations of earth, strange pictures carved on a rock ledge, or curious objects found while plowing. They and "amateur archaeologists" (citizens who collect artifacts as a hobby) are often interviewed by archaeologists working in a region. This process of "collector interview" can provide much information on the location and identification of archaeological sites. Both the individual farmer or collector and the archaeologist benefit from such interaction.

Finally, archaeological sites are sometimes discovered by accident—a road bank might cut through a site, a person digging a foundation for a house might unearth some artifacts, or natural processes such as wind and erosion might expose a previously buried site. When these accidents occur, it is important to report these finds to professional archaeologists so that the information can be properly recorded and documented. If at all possible, contact the archaeologist before the remains are pulled out of the ground or before the area is filled in, so that the archaeologist can properly record the context of the find.

Dating Sites — Determining "How Old?"

"How old is it?" is a natural question to ask an archaeologist. In Wisconsin, there is evidence that people have settled here for the last 10,000-12,000 years. Since it is often surprising to learn how long people have been living in Wiscosin, perhaps another question that should be addressed is "How do you know how old it is?"

Many people have heard of radiocarbon or C-14 dating, but archaeologists also use other techniques for determining the age of an archaeological site. Radiocarbon dating is based on the fact that all living things collect and store a certain amount of carbon. When the plant or animal dies, no more carbon accumulates. One part of the carbon stored is called carbon-14 (C-14). The C-14 begins to decay at a known, fixed rate at the death of the plant or animal, so scientists can measure the amount of C-14 left, and calculate the time which has elapsed since death. Radiocarbon dating can be done only on preserved organic materials. Radiocarbon dating is of critical importance to archaeology, but not every site provides a situation where adequate samples for radiocarbon dates can be collected. Even when C-14 samples can be collected, archaeologists use C-14 dating *plus* a variety of other techniques to help answer the question "how old."

Dating techniques can be divided into two types: relative and chronometric. A relative dating technique is one which is used to determine that A is older or younger than B. The technique does not provide a date in years, just the age of one thing *relative* to another. While not immediately impressive,

8

Shovel probe survey at equal intervals. These students are spaced at five-meter intervals. Each shovel probe is carefully examined for evidence of prehistoric occupation.

most of the "how old" questions are answered by means of relative dating techniques. An example may help clarify the process. Compare the State Capitol Building in Madison and the Performing Arts Center (PAC) in Milwaukee. Using general knowledge about styles and architecture, we would say that the State Capitol Building is older. If we knew exactly when the State Capitol Building was built, we'd know that that was the oldest that the PAC could date. Then, if we found a slightly newer building, we could gradually close in on a date for the PAC. Of course, in this case we could check the cornerstones, but such help is not available in sites of pre-literate peoples. Knowing relative age is very helpful, and once the sequence is documented, the technique can help to determine a more precise age for everything else.

A chronometric dating technique provides a date in years (i.e., so many years ago), which can be translated into B.C. or A.D. People used to call such techniques "absolute" dating techniques, but this label is misleading since the date is far from absolute. The date provided by a chronometric technique is actually a range — for example, A.D. 1000 ± 100. The number doesn't mean that the actual date is A.D. 1000, but rather that the chances are two out of three that the correct date is between A.D. 900 and A.D. 1100. These dates are approximations or likely ranges, and this is the reason that archaeologists try to get a number of dates from a particular occupation — if all the sample dates cluster around the same date, it is more likely that that date is accurate. Radiocarbon dating is the most common of the chronometric

techniques, especially in Wisconsin, but it is by no means the only one.

Both types of dating techniques have their advantages and disadvantages, but both are critical for archaeology and both are regularly used. Archaeologists try, in fact, to use as many techniques as possible to insure the most accurate dates for their sites.

Most commonly, archaeologists count on two relative dating techniques for basic age determination of a site. These two techniques are stratigraphy and cross-dating. Stratigraphy is based on the principle that older things are generally deeper in the ground than more recent materials. By examining the layers, or strata, of occupation on an archaeological site, one can determine which is earliest, latest, and so on. By carefully correlating this information with any chronometric dates one might have, the general time ranges of the cultures can be determined.

For cross-dating, archaeologists depend upon horizon markers or diagnostic artifacts. These are items which have distinctive characteristics and are always found in a particular society. Examples include things such as pottery styles, projectile point types, and so on. These markers provide clues to the time period and/or specific culture represented. When materials are dated with chronometric techniques, detailed context is recorded. In this way, firm dates can be associated with certain diagnostics or markers. Then, when these characteristic items are found again on another site with no chronometric dates, they can be assigned to the same time period as the dated items. Obviously, the more confirming chronometric dates one has, the more certain the general assignments. Cross-dating is the method which allows an archaeologist to look at a particular artifact type and assign it to a particular time period/or culture.

"How old is it?" is not easy to answer. All of the methods used have disadvantages and problems, and archaeologists are continually looking for new techniques and better methods for dating materials. Archaeologists have generally answered the "how old" question fairly well, but remember that all of the answers are approximate, and, in some cases, may vary by as much as a few hundred years. Of course, since archaeologists generally deal with periods of hundreds or even thousands of years, fluctuation by a hundred or so years is not quite so bad.

The general prehistoric time periods which archaeologists recognize for Wisconsin are presented in the following list.

Paleo-Indian
    10,000-8500 B.C.
Archaic
Early Archaic	8500-6000 B.C.
Middle Archaic	6000-3000 B.C.
Late Archaic	3000-1000 B.C.
Woodland
Early Woodland	1000-300 B.C.
Middle Woodland	300 B.C.-A.D. 400
Late Woodland	A.D. 400-1100
Mississippian
Middle Mississippian	A.D. 1000-1500
Upper Mississippian	A.D. 1000-1500

Subsequent chapters of this book are organized according to these divisions. These divisions have been created by archaeologists, based on certain horizon markers and other similarities. Each time period will probably include more than one specific culture; the division into specific cultures may not always be clearly indicated in the archaeological record. It is important to remember that these categories are arbitrary divisions made by archaeologists, and that there were no people who called themselves Paleo-Indian or Archaic. Also, you will note that there is overlap between the different time periods — some of the different traditions overlapped and existed at the same times.

Archaeologists are not generally able to tell which of these prehistoric groups might be ancestors to modern Wisconsin tribes. Making such determinations is extremely difficult and requires much more information than is currently available. Some archaeologists think that the Winnebago tribe might be descended from an Upper Mississippian culture known as the Oneota, but other archaeologists have questioned this conclusion — unfortunately, there is evidence for both arguments, and we may never know the real answer. Regardless of who the ancient Indian's modern descendants might be, archaeologists have been able to learn quite a bit about each of the prehistoric time periods listed here.

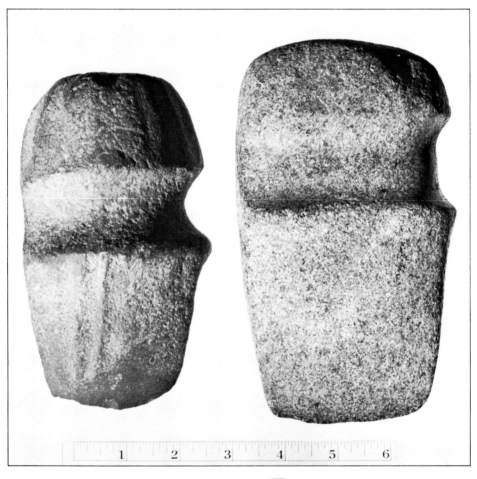

Ground stone tools. Left, fluted axe; right, grooved axe.

Sharpening stone. The piece of sandstone shows the effects of having been used for implement sharpening.

Technology:
Tool Manufacture and Use

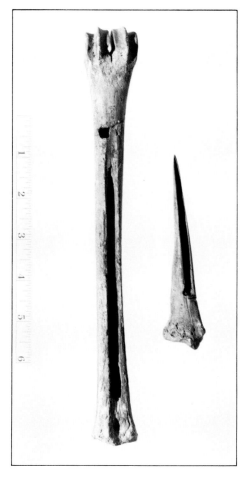

Bone tools. Left, a beaming tool made from a deer leg bone used to scrape hides. An awl is on the right.

Before we begin discussion of the specifics of Wisconsin's prehistory, it is useful to examine some basics of prehistoric technology so that we can more easily understand the significance of the items later described. Technology is the way people use their environment to meet their needs. Understanding technology includes an understanding of how tools are made and used.

Sometimes archaeologists find evidence of houses, and sometimes the presence of houses can be inferred from the patterns of stains and artifacts found on an archaeological site. For example, if we find some remnants of posts laid out in a rectangle, and within that rectangle we find evidence of a hearth, some broken pottery and perhaps some other items, we might suggest that the pattern of items probably represents a house. Many prehistoric activities can be inferred from the patterns and kinds of artifacts found in the ground. More often, however, archaeologists find only the debris — the preserved garbage left from everyday prehistoric life.

While it would be difficult to discuss all of the things that archaeologists can determine from a site, it might be helpful to review some of the things we can infer, and how we can determine them.

If a whole artifact is found, its use can sometimes be determined by analogy — comparing it to something similar documented for another group. Sometimes, use can be determined by context, but usually a combination of analogy, context, comparison to what is already known, and common sense is used. In certain cases, archaeologists can carefully examine the artifact and tell *how* it has been used. An example

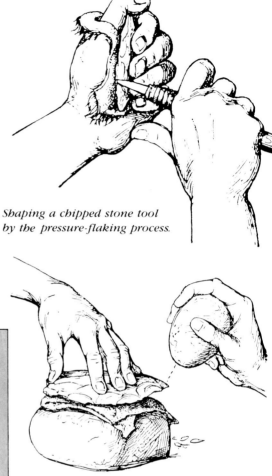

Shaping a chipped stone tool by the pressure-flaking process.

Hammerstone shows one end abraded from use.

Shaping a chipped stone tool by percussion flaking.

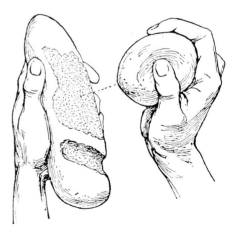

Shaping a ground stone axe by the pecking process.

here would include microscopic examination of the edges of tools. While most people call the generally triangular points found in fields all over Wisconsin "arrowheads," archaeologists call them "projectile points." Why? Because archaeologists, through the study of technology, have learned two things: 1) examination of the edges of these artifacts indicate that many of these items were used as knives or spears or other tools, and *not* as arrows; and 2) the bow and arrow was apparently not used in Wisconsin until the Late Woodland period.

Archaeologists find a lot more than pots and points. We also find scrapers, drills, axes, and especially flakes. Flakes are simply bits and pieces of debris which are chipped off when making an arrow or point or other artifact from stone. These chips can tell us a lot about the people's technology, since they were often used as tools, and since we can sometimes tell what kind of technique was used to make them. Most prehistoric chipped stone artifacts were made of chert or flint, with some being made from quartzite, quartz, and other materials. Chert is the easiest of these materials to work, but especially in northern Wisconsin, chert was not very commonly found.

Prehistoric people used two basic techniques in manufacturing chipped stone artifacts: percussion flaking and pressure flaking. Throughout the prehistory of Wisconsin both techniques were used, but the degree to which each was used varied with the geographic area, the time period, the raw materials, and the kinds of artifacts being made.

Percussion flaking involves hitting one stone with another — chips are usually struck off by hitting the raw material with a rounded stone called a hammerstone. Sometimes, if a smaller flake is desired, the raw material is hit with something softer, like an antler or bone; this creates a smaller, thinner, less blocky flake. Most prehistoric artifacts were produced by percussion flaking, and the toolmaker controlled the result by varying the force of the blow and by using different kinds of "hammerstones" to strike off flakes.

For very fine work, prehistoric craftspeople might have used the technique of pressure flaking, where flakes are "squeezed" off by applying pressure with an antler tip or sharpened bone. This technique was usually reserved for finishing an artifact or creating a specific kind of edge.

By carefully examining the flakes left on an archaeological site, the archaeologist can usually determine if those flakes were produced by percussion or pressure flaking, and new techniques even allow us to determine how the flake may have been used. New methods of analysis suggest that it is possible to tell whether, for example, the edge of a flake was used on grass, dried hide, meat, bone, and so on.

Some stone artifacts were not made by chipping. Things like axes and adzes, grooved for attaching a handle, were made by another process called "pecking and polishing," or "pecking and grinding." Instead of being chipped stone tools, these tools are called *ground stone* tools. A stone was shaped into an artifact by continuously pounding on it with another stone to remove particles by pulverization. The artifact was then finished by rubbing it with a piece of abrasive stone until a smooth polish was obtained.

Chipped stone implements include drills (top) and projectile points (bottom).

Stone tools are by far the most common kinds of artifacts found, but artifacts were also made from bone, pottery, and copper. Items made from wood were probably more common, but are not often preserved in climates like Wisconsin's. Bone artifacts include things like awls, harpoons, needles, and even bone flutes. Pottery which was made into drinking, cooking, and storage vessels, as well as figurines and pipes, was made only since the Woodland period, and will be discussed in that section of the book. Copper was almost the only metal used in prehistoric Wisconsin, and copper was made into knives, awls, points, harpoons, fishhooks, bracelets, and beads.

One final kind of "artifact" should also be mentioned. This "artifact" type includes rock carvings and cave paintings. Most people think of cave paintings as something found only in France, but the people who lived in Wisconsin also practiced this art form. Cave or rock paintings (using some sort of pigment) are called *pictographs,* and rock or cave carvings (for which someone actually incises the rock) are called *petroglyphs.* Both types of drawings occur in Wisconsin, and they are fascinating because they offer a glimpse into the aesthetic realm of what people did. We guess that some of the drawings relate directly to hunting and the animals which were important for daily life, but it is also likely that as many drawings were directly related to ceremonial and spiritual concerns. These drawings, while fascinating, are also problematic. It is difficult to date them and to relate them to specific sites and cultures, and it is rare that we have the opportunity to understand their full context.

Bone implements. Top, mesh spreader of turtle bone used to make fish nets; bottom, harpoon.

Flotation setup at Aztalan excavations in 1984. Dirt is poured into the large drum. Water pressure is used to float and separate materials from the dirt. The plant remains — lightest in weight — are carried off the end of the spout and are caught in the small mesh screen. Other remains are captured in a screen inside the barrel.

Environment and Diet

This is a close-up of the small screen in the flotation process which catches the lighter weight plant remains.

Reconstructing the environment

Archaeologists have long been aware of the importance of the environment on the location of human settlement. The importance of landforms, water resources, and vegetation has been particularly clear in Wisconsin. What was the environment like in prehistoric times? Was it the same during all of prehistory, or did it change? If so, what was it like when? How do archaeologists reconstruct the environment of prehistoric people?

Although we can get some idea of the environment from the remains of what people ate, we need a broader picture, since people tend to be selective about what they eat. One of the better ways to determine prehistoric environment is through the study of pollen — those same minute particles that cause so many people trouble during the summer months.

The analysis of plant pollen and spores is known as palynology. Most plants shed their pollen into the atmosphere, where it is rapidly dispersed by wind action. Pollen grains are present in most of the earth's atmosphere, including archaeological sites. Further, these pollen grains are generally preserved in the earth for thousands and thousands of years. It is not surprising that pollen grains are abundant, since a single pine branch produces as many as 350 million pollen grains.

Pollen samples are samples of earth taken from the profile or wall of test pits or trenches, or from bogs or other wetlands. Special care is taken to prevent contamination from foreign or modern pollen. Samples are taken through all deposits to provide a continous record. The pollen grains are isolated in the laboratory and a sample of the many grains identified. The results are converted to percentages of kinds of plants for each level, and the proportional shift in kinds of plants between levels can be seen.

The pollen diagram can be compared with those for living plant communities. The ratio of tree to non-tree pollen, for example, generally indicates the degree of forest present. When pollen percentages fluctuate through time, one can interpret shifts in prehistoric habitats and climate.

Once several pollen diagrams from an area have been integrated, a regional sequence can be constructed. At this point, broad patterns can be discovered and interpreted. Because pollen is so abundant and travels so far, it provides a large-scale picture of what an area's environment was like.

Pollen is only one means by which archaeologists reconstruct the prehistoric environment. Other kinds of information are used as well, including data from geology, physical geography, and historic records. During the 1830s and 1840s, the territory which includes present-day Wisconsin was surveyed by the U.S. General Land Office in order to divide the land for sale to farmers and homesteaders. These surveys resulted in our current land system of townships and sections, but the surveyor's notes also provide invaluable information on the state's early environment. The surveyors noted the vegetation as they measured out land parcels, and they marked a "witness tree" every mile. By reading through the notes and maps, we can reconstruct the different vegetation zones which existed at that time (before farming and towns and roads changed everything). Botanists

and others have determined that these reconstructions are probably pretty accurate estimates of what the vegetation looked like for the last 5000 years. In Wisconsin, this 5000-year period includes many of the known prehistoric cultures.

By pooling information from a variety of sources, archaeologists reconstruct a prehistoric environment and how it might have changed through time. This reconstruction allows the archaeologist to determine what was available to eat, and then that information can be compared to what was actually selected by the prehistoric inhabitants. While archaeological sites are often found in present-day cornfields, it is important to determine what the land was like long ago in order to understand the setting, and what that site may have represented.

Determining Prehistoric Diets

An important aspect of archaeological analysis deals with *subsistence* — quite simply, how do people get their groceries and what groceries do they eat? Generally, there are two lines of evidence from which we infer prehistoric diet. One is primary evidence — the actual remains of foodstuffs, and the other is secondary evidence — items that suggest a particular type of food or food-getting strategy.

Primary evidence most often includes faunal and floral remains — bits and pieces of plants and animals which are preserved on archaeological sites. These remains can be identified by comparison to bones from animals whose species and age are known, or to plants or plant parts whose species are known. In other words, comparative collections of known materials are used

A "floated" sample. On the left are animal remains, on the right, plant remains. These remains provide detailed information on what prehistoric people ate.

to identify the unknown. This process is often tedious and difficult since the remains are usually small and fragmentary. A good knowledge of comparative zoology and botany is necessary to properly identify these materials.

Broken animal bones can provide direct evidence of which species were hunted or collected, how animals were captured, and how they were butchered. Sometimes one can determine how many animals were killed at a time and how much meat was consumed. Bones and shell can also give us information on seasonality — the time of year during which sites were inhabited.

Plant remains can provide direct evidence of which plants were collected, and how the various plants were prepared. Unfortunately, plant gathering and agriculture are almost always underrepresented at archaeological sites, because the tiny seeds and other plant parts that result from activities like food storage, grinding, and harvesting are among the most fragile of all archaeological remains. Unless preservation is excellent, or the plant remains are charred, remnants of plants used in prehistoric times are not often found. To recover whatever tiny plant and animal remains are present, archaeologists use a technique known as flotation. Flotation uses water or chemicals and fine screens to free the tiny seeds and animal remains from the soil. The plant remains float to the top and the animal remains float higher than things like small rocks or pieces of pottery.

Flotation is a process which was first described in 1968; it became very popular during the 1970s, and is considered by most archaeologists to be mandatory in any excavation. The results from flotation have dramatically altered our interpretations of prehistoric economies. Because many of these small remains were not even seen before, archaeologists developed ideas of prehistoric economy based only on what they could see. Deer and other animal bone were identified from sites, but it was rare that archaeologists knew that prehistoric people relied as much on various small fish and plants, nuts, and berries. Older interpretations generally ignored the question of plant use, largely because plant remains were seldom found. Flotation has enabled us to create a more realistic picture of prehistoric subsistence.

Human bone can also provide clues to diet and nutrition. Bones tell the story of diet, and certain diseases and microscopic and trace element analysis can indicate the kinds of foods which were eaten. Studies of bone chemistry, for example, have only been possible within the last few years — now, even small pieces of human bone can indicate what people were eating. In addition, evidence of cavities and tooth wear patterns can suggest the kinds of foods or the amount of carbohydrates in the diet.

Secondary evidence for subsistence is more common, and is the kind of evidence that most people know about — things like tools, kind of house, and prehistoric art. As discussed above, new techniques for examining the used edge of certain tool types can even suggest the kind of material on which the tool was used — for example, hides, plants, meat, wood, bone, etc. Archaeologists must now incorporate all of these different types of evidence to get a picture of what people were actually eating, and compare this to what was available.

The Environment of Prehistoric Wisconsin

The first evidence we have for people living in the state of Wisconsin coincides with the melting and retreat of the last glacier, about 12,000 B.C. Wisconsin looked much different then — it looked similar to parts of Canada and Alaska today, with sparse vegetation and cold climate. The weather eventually warmed up, and as the glaciers retreated further and further north, Wisconsin came to resemble its current vegetation patterns.

The northern part of the state tends to be cooler and moister than the southern part of the state; likewise, northern Wisconsin tends to have more pine trees, spruce, and aspen than southern Wisconsin. Southern Wisconsin is warmer and drier, with more oak, maple, hickory, and basswood trees. There is a transitional zone between these two extremes, with some of both types of vegetation. Although the climate changed at various stages during prehistory, there was generally a similar sort of difference between the northern and southern portions of the state.

While the main vegetation differences in Wisconsin are north to south, there are also differences we can see from east to west. The level of Lake Michigan changed at various times in prehistory, and more or less land was exposed for prehistoric habitation. The eastern part of the state is more level and is made up of more rolling hills, swamps, and gentle rivers than the western part of the state. This difference is largely the result of the glaciers, because the weight and size of the glaciers caused a general leveling of the landscape. Since the last glaciation did not effect parts of western Wisconsin, the terrain is much more rugged and dissected. These differences have an affect on what people will do for food, since the differences in vegetation, climate, and terrain will affect what plants and animals will be present. In subsequent discussions, we will try to note differences in prehistoric adaptations in different parts of the state.

23

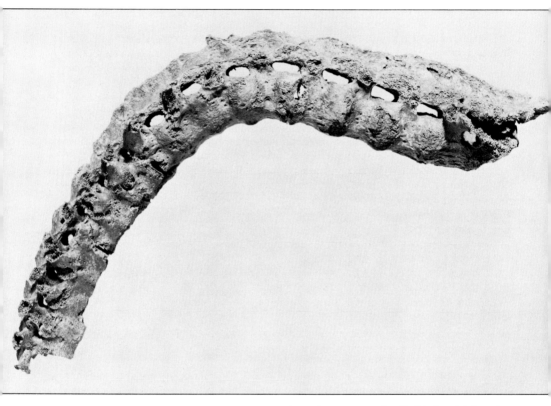

*An extreme case of arthritis in which verte-
brae of the backbone have been fused.*

Human Biology

Many of the early excavations in Wisconsin focused on burial mounds and other mortuary sites. A number of skeletons were recovered, but few people realized how much information can be gained from the study of human bone.

A summary of the kinds of information we can learn by studying human bone includes:

1. Demographic and population information, including age and sex of the individuals.

2. Health information, including diet, nutrition, disease and pathologies.

3. Genetic relationships.

4. Social organization.

5. Economic and political structure.

Archaeologists and biological anthropologists can gather demographic and population information from burials because the age and sex of many burials can be determined by careful examination of the bones. Prehistoric population profiles can be compared to modern populations of known size and type; estimates can be made from these data about the number of people who may have been present at the site or the area, and the length of time the site may have been occupied. These data can also be used to determine whether the individuals buried at the site make up a normal profile — that is, are females or males or individuals of a certain age under- or over-represented?

Burials can provide much information on health. Certain diseases, such as some types of diet deficiencies, will be evident in the bones. As an example, recent analysis of some human bone from a Late Woodland site in Wisconsin clearly indicates that the individual had tuberculosis. The presence of tuberculosis is especially interesting since it generally occurs in situations where people are living relatively close together. Similarly, arthritis is commonly found in prehistoric populations, and careful study of arthritis patterning may allow one to determine whether different work patterns or different kinds of work were performed by different people.

Careful examination of teeth can also lead to important information about diet; dental pathologies and patterns of caries indicate what people were eating. We can also note whether medical practices included tending to broken bones. In a few cases, health and medical practice can be determined quite literally. In one particular Wisconsin instance originally cited by Ritzenthaler, an arrow was found embedded in a lumbar vertebra, piercing the spinal column to the extent that the individual must have been paralyzed from the waist down. Evidence of bone healing on this wound demonstrated that the victim must have remained alive for at least a year after he was wounded, and the people were able and willing to maintain a handicapped person.

Some techniques which tell us about the health and diet of a population are relatively new. Detailed radiographs can provide information on the regularity and consistency of diet. In earlier years, archaeologists thought that bits and fragments of bone could yield little to no information on the population being studied. Today, however, bits of bone can be subjected to trace element analysis to help determine diet, and bone chemistry studies can determine whether the individuals ate a diet based on cultivated grains such as corn, or one heavier in meat products. Studies done on some of the human bones from

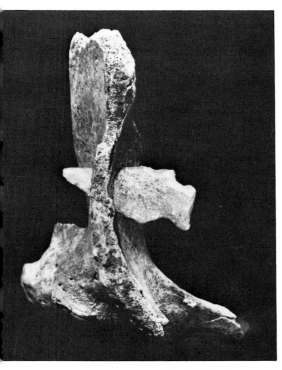

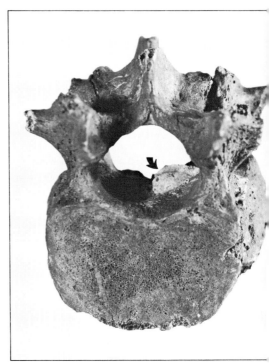

Arrow embedded in bone.   *Arrowhead embedded in vertebra.*

the Aztalan site, for example, confirm that these people ate maize.

Genetic relationships can be examined in human burial populations when one has a large enough sample. There are certain characteristics or traits on bone which are inherited; these traits can be calculated for entire populations, and the degree of genetic relationship between two or more groups, as well as the homogeneity of relationships within a particular group, can be estimated.

Burials can often aid in the determination of the relationship of one group of burials to another. Just as the use of space is important in life, the use of space also has meaning in death. Sometimes, immediate family or other kin groups are indicated by the placement of burials, and one can determine some of the basic organizational principles of the society being studied. Characteristics like positioning, orientation, number and kind of grave goods, etc., can provide information on the organization of the society being studied.

Finally, in terms of economics and political structure, burials can be used to identify whether or not there are high status or leadership positions within a society, and if so, what individuals are in those positions. Sometimes, items like grave goods can also indicate division of labor — noting that certain items are buried only with men or women.

In sum, there are many things which can only be learned by studying burials; the information is not generally represented in other kinds of archaeological features.

This lower leg bone shows the result of fracture and mending.

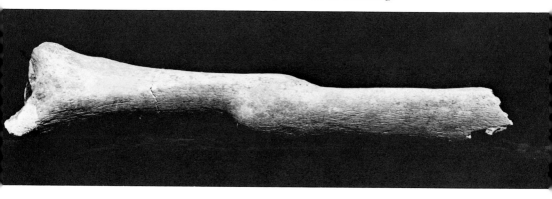

Characteristic projectile point of the Paleo-Indian period. Note that most of the points have a "flute" running up from the base. This made hafting easier.

The Paleo-Indian People:
Wisconsin's First Settlers

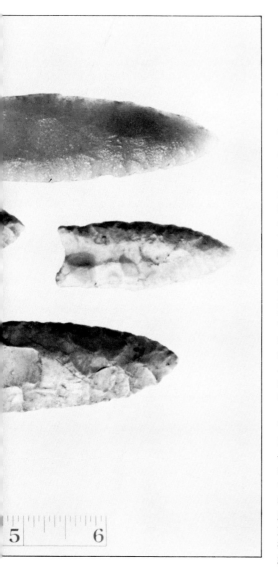

Where did Wisconsin's earliest residents come from? The earliest immigrants into the New World are thought to have come from Asia at various times throughout the last "Ice Age," called the Pleistocene. The ice sheets, or glaciers, covered huge land masses, and contained tons of water. The amount of water frozen in the glaciers meant that sea levels were lowered and land that was previously under water was now exposed. One such area is now called the Bering Straits, and is a narrow band of water separating northeastern Siberia from western Alaska. Evidence suggest that at several times during the Pleistocene, the straits emerged as dry land. This strip of land has been called a "land bridge" (it is also sometimes known as Beringia), but it was hundreds of miles wide. Plants, animals, and humans came across this "bridge" at various times, and continued into the rest of North America because parts of Alaska apparently remained ice-free during these times.

Archaeologists call these early "immigrants" — the people who lived here from about 10,000 B.C.-8500 B.C. — Paleo-Indians. We don't know a lot about Paleo-Indian cultures because very little is left of their camps. The small, scattered bands of hunters, groups of maybe twenty-five to thirty, probably entered the region from the south after the retreat of the last glaciers. The Paleo-Indian people made their way south and east from Alaska, across the Plains, then north to Wisconsin over a period of many years. Because these people moved often and were gathered in relatively small groups, they did not often leave permanent traces of their lifeway behind. Most evidence for the Paleo-Indian time period comes from the West, with some newer data from the East and Southeast. The earliest residents of Wisconsin probably led very similar lives; the same kinds of fluted points and other artifacts are found on all Paleo-Indian sites.

The Wisconsin of 10,000-11,000 B.C. was much different than today; it was colder, and the last remnants of the glaciers were melting and retreating northward. Northern Wisconsin had sections of tundra, and in southern Wisconsin there were the beginnings of forests of spruce and fir, with scattered swamps. This type of environment could probably provide food to small bands of hunters, gatherers, and foragers.

Archaeologists have assumed that these citizens were big game hunters — hunters of mammoths and mastodons (extinct forms of elephants). Some Paleo-Indian spear points have been found with remains of these extinct animals in states south and west of Wisconsin, and since few other kinds of sites have been found, people have concluded that big game was the major subsistence focus. The Paleo-Indian people were probably primarily dependent upon large game animals such as barren ground caribou, mammoth, and musk-ox, although many smaller species were probably utilized as well. These large animals preferred well-drained areas, and we frequently find Paleo-Indian projectile points as isolated finds in upland areas, along old lake shores, or on high terraces or river and stream valleys. Most artifacts which are known to date to this period, however, are found scattered without any clear indication of what these

people did. Recent excavations on Paleo-Indian sites in other northeastern states have suggested that big game was only one part of these people's lives, and that because of problems of preservation, we are not necessarily getting a complete picture of what Paleo-Indian people did for a living.

Relatively few Paleo-Indian sites have been recorded for Wisconsin, with most sites yielding a characteristic Paleo-Indian point and maybe a few flakes and tools, rather than a clear Paleo-Indian habitation. However, the high till plains and wetland strips within the state would have been ideal for the kinds of game pursued, and we have some evidence that these people inhabited Wisconsin for some period of time.

The Paleo-Indian tradition is characterized by a distinctive kind of projectile point, called a "fluted" point. Examples of fluted points are indicated in several of the photographs, and consist of a roughly triangular-shaped chipped stone point with a long flute or groove extending upward from the base. This flute is present on one or both sides of the point. The flute was apparently made by carefully pressure-flaking a long thin flake from the base of the point after the rest of the point was completed. The two types of fluted points are Clovis and Folsom. On a Clovis point, the flute extends only part-way up the side, but on a Folsom point the flute extends almost the entire length of the point. Clovis points are far more common in Wisconsin. Besides fluted points, these people made and used end scrapers, small flake knives, abraders, choppers, rubbing stones, and what is thought to be an engraving tool called a "graver." As seen in the photographs of the gravers, they are scrapers with a distinctive "spur" on the working edge. We think that these spurs were used to work and incise bone. While gravers have been found in other contexts, they are often considered diagnostic of the Paleo-Indian period.

We don't have much detail about the Paleo-Indian way of life. Many of the known Paleo-Indian artifacts were apparently used in processing game and dressing hides. We know almost nothing about Paleo-Indian perishable goods, housing, religion or social organization, but some assumptions based on what we do know can be made. Further west, there is evidence for group hunting parties, with individuals banding together to trap and kill certain game animals. This kind of activity required some level of cooperation and social control to succeed. Since Paleo-Indian people tended to move fairly often, housing was probably temporary, involving a bone or wood frame covered with animal skins, or small camps in caves and rockshelters. People probably dressed in animal skins, and we think that they ate and used plants as well as animals. These people did not have bows and arrows, they were not gardeners, and they did not make pottery. The different climate and vegetation of Wisconsin at the time led to a distinctive lifestyle.

Why don't we know more about our first residents? When people move frequently, they leave little garbage behind for us to find; second, erosion and farming destroy remains; and third, areas like this one with a lot of moisture don't preserve things as well as dry places like deserts. Hopefully, archaeologists in Wisconsin will some

day be able to excavate a well preserved Paleo-Indian site to learn more about the early citizens of the state.

A clovis projectile point on the left, and two "gravers." The distinctive sharp graver points may have been used for engraving bone.

The Archaic Populations:
Hunters, Gatherers, and Fishermen

The next period of Wisconsin's prehistory is known as the Archaic, and it is divided into three parts: *Early Archaic* dates from 8500-6000 B.C., *Middle Archaic* from 6000-3000 B.C., and *Late Archaic* from 3000-1000 B.C. Some archaeologists combine the Early Archaic with late Paleo-Indian, and discuss a separate "Late Paleo-Indian" period. For simplicity, we will restrict our discussion of Paleo-Indian to those people who made and used fluted points. Some of the things discussed here as Early Archaic would be called Late Paleo-Indian by other archaeologists.

If you compare this chapter with the 1953 version of this book, you will discover that in 1953 there was almost no mention of the Archaic, especially the Early and Middle Archaic. The only Archaic groups mentioned were the "Old Copper People" and the "Red Ocher People," both specific manifestations of the Late Archaic period and known only from mortuary sites. Today, however, there is information from a variety of different kinds of Archaic sites, as well as detailed subsistence evidence recovered by means of the flotation process.

The Archaic period immediately follows the Paleo-Indian period, but continues for a very long period of time, about 7500 years. Unlike the Paleo-Indian period, there are many Archaic sites of different types throughout Wisconsin. At the beginning of the Archaic period, the climate was colder than it is now, but it gradually became more moderate. The forests were conifer (evergreen or pine trees) and were like the forest we now see in northern Wisconsin and Canada; however, in southern Wisconsin and lower Michigan, deciduous trees (oak,

2

4

7

Copper implements: (1) awl (2) socketed-tang spear point (3) rat-tail spear point (4) socketed axe (5) fish hook (6) serrate-tang point (7) knive (8) conical point (9) crescent knife (10) harpoon.

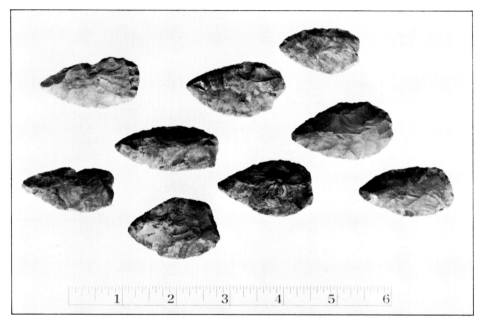

Ovate trianguloid knives.

Red ocher type blade found covered with red ocher in Milwaukee County.

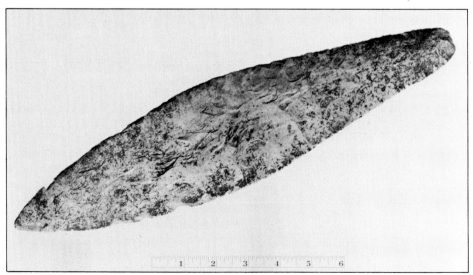

maple, hickory) became more common. Hunting probably provided the major food source, although some fishing was probably done during the summer, and nuts and other plant foods took on increasing importance. The major game animals were probably moose, woodland caribou, beaver, hare, and especially deer.

The climate continued to warm, and people in this part of the Great Lakes counted on deer hunting, although around 6000 B.C. there was an increase in emphasis on other resources. Ground stone tools, things like axes and grinding stones, first appear during the Archaic, and it is clear that plant foods became a more important part of the diet. Throughout the Archaic, the deciduous forests — the oaks, maples, and hickories — became more widespread, and provided a greater and richer variety of food resources.

For the Archaic period as a whole, we can begin to examine settlement, subsistence, technology, religion, and social organization because there are many reported sites, there have been a number of excavations conducted, and the record of Archaic peoples remains relatively well preserved. Population increased throughout the Archaic period, and people began to settle into territories and stay in one place longer. Changes in the environment were probably one part of the reason for increased population and a more sedentary existence — the new environments could support more people with more and richer food resources.

The Early Archaic period is largely a continuation of the Paleo-Indian way of life. The climate became more moderate than in the Paleo-Indian period, and important game animals were probably moose, woodland caribou, beaver, hare, and, where available, deer. Hunting was probably still the major subsistence activity, although some fishing may have been practiced. Early Archaic sites are especially common in the southern half of the state where the deciduous forests became a common place to find deer. Like the previous Paleo-Indian period, sites are frequently no more than isolated finds in upland areas and other similar locales. Also like the Paleo-Indian period, we know little of the details of the Early Archaic way of life, and little about actual site distributions, subsistence-settlement patterns, or social organization. One difference between the Early Archaic and the Paleo-Indian period is that there is more diversity in Early Archaic projectile point styles and types. Archaeologists have suggested that these differences may represent the first real signs of regionalization. After the glaciers moved northward, the climate warmed, our current vegetation patterns began to emerge, and people found that a variety of different foods were now available in different places and that the best strategy was to adapt food-getting to the particular location. With this shift in strategy, people developed a variety of different artifact styles, reflecting the beginnings of regional patterns of adaptation.

The Middle Archaic period dates from about 6000-3000 B.C. The climate became even milder, and part of the Middle Archaic coincides with the peak of a warmer and drier period when the climate was warmer than today. People in Wisconsin still had an economy based on deer hunting, but with greater emphasis on other resources. Ground stone tools appear in quantities for the first time, and plant resources (especially things like nuts) became more important. The greater distribution of the deciduous forest during this time yielded a wider variety of exploitable resources. Recent work in Illinois has expanded our knowledge of the Middle Archaic, but no major excavations concentrating on this time period have yet been done in Wisconsin. The Illinois evidence suggests an increase in social complexity, indications of the beginnings of trade, and burial in simple individual graves.

The portion of the Archaic period from about 3000-1000 B.C. is known as the Late Archaic. This time period provides evidence for clear and different regional traditions throughout the Great Lakes region.

In northern Wisconsin during the Late Archaic period, people followed a winter hunting/summer fishing economy. Traditionally these people, concentrated in the upper third of the state, have been known as the "Old Copper Culture." The so-called "Old Copper Culture" name is derived from the extensive use of copper artifacts by these people. The copper was extracted from the Lake Superior area and shaped by cold hammering or heating and hammering. Artifact types include knives, awls, spear points, projectile points, axes, harpoons, fishhooks, and a variety of ornaments. Most of the Old Copper specimens come from burial contexts, and it is now thought that, rather than representing some distinct culture, people in this part of the state during the Late Archaic period used copper and buried it with their dead as a part of their ceremonialism. Copper is also found in other contexts, but its

A gorget ornament left, bow-tie banner stone from Osceola site, right.

36

Banner stones.

37

Turkey-tail points.

widest expression seems to be in mortuary ritual. Other items found with these Old Copper burials include finely chipped projectile points and spears and bannerstones.

The bannerstone is an important artifact in the Late Archaic period, suggesting development of a new hunting technique. Often associated with Late Archaic sites throughout the Great Lakes region, bannerstones come in a variety of shapes; all are heavy, ground stone with a drilled hole or perforation. Archaeologists believe bannerstones may have been used as weights on an "atlatl" or spear thrower. An atlatl is a wooden shaft about two feet long, fitted with a hook at one end and a handle at the other. Bannerstones or other weights may also have fitted onto this shaft. The shaft was then used to propel the spear, giving the hunter greater leverage and greater force. The bannerstone would have acted as a counter-balance for greater lever action.

In southern Wisconsin, the economy was based on winter deer hunting, spring and summer fishing, *and* collection of a wide variety of plant foods (especially wild nuts and seeds). This diverse resource base required regular, planned movement between resources, and probably regular territories within which settlements were moved to exploit these resources. Widespread exchange networks began to develop during the Late Archaic period, and it is believed these networks might have started because of differential availability of resources within these territories. People began to trade for things they needed that their own territories did not include. Sites are found in many different kinds

of areas, demonstrating that seasonal exploitation of resources was important. Burial traditions and rituals — like burial mounds — began during this period.

In southern Wisconsin, archaeologists defined what was called the "Red Ocher" and "Glacial Kame" cultures. Like "Old Copper," these cultures were defined from a specific way of treating the dead. In the case of Red Ocher, the burials were capped with powdered ocher, which colored the burial red. These burials usually consisted of a few individuals interred in a flexed position in sand or gravel, with some chipped-stone points or blades. A common chipped stone artifact found with these burials is the so-called "turkey-tail" point of bluish-gray chert. The points are called "turkey-tails" because of the resemblance of the hafting end to the tail of a dressed turkey. Also distinctive are large, white ceremonial chipped stone blades which were sometimes deliberately broken or presumably "killed" for use in the next world — a custom still observed by some people today. These Red Ocher burials may also contain some copper, especially beads and awls, as well as shell beads, galena (lead) cubes, and polished stone tube pipes, birdstones, or gorgets.

"Glacial Kame" culture also referred to a specific manner of burying the dead. The "culture" was so-named from a series of burials in gravel knolls. The burials had marine shell ornaments, beads, and gorgets. "Glacial Kame" was thought to slightly precede "Red Ocher" in age, and be a forerunner for it.

Although terms like Old Copper, Red Ocher, and Glacial Kame describe some of the differences found in mortuary ritual within the Late Archaic period, it is very difficult to assign such terms to habitation sites or ways of life. Archaeologists generally no longer use the terms to describe different cultures. Copper was found in all three "cultures," and each only provides an idea about differences in treatment of the dead, not differences in way of life or subsistence. What is clear from all three of these "cultures" is that Late Archaic people began to "build" communal burial facilities with more elaborate ceremonialism. This degree of effort suggest that the Late Archaic burial practices may be a forerunner for the elaborate mounds and tombs of the Middle Woodland period. Late Archaic burial grounds may actually represent territorial markers, especially since their appearance coincides with the first real evidence of prehistoric territoriality.

Prior to the Late Archaic, the climate was in continuous change and the resources available differed from period to period. By the time of the Late Archaic period, however, the climate had stabilized and the environment was not significantly different from our own. In fact, recent studies suggest that Late Archaic settlement patterns (at least in the southern portion of the state) are very similar to prehistoric Woodland patterns (see the next chapter) and historic Woodland Indian patterns. A large part of the reason for this similarity in patterning is probably the similar environment.

The long Archaic period was *prior* to the development of pottery, agriculture, and the bow and arrow. However, these people were well adapted to their environment, and by the end of the Archaic, had a complex social system with trade (including copper from northern Wisconsin), and clear traditions and rituals. Population increased steadily, and people's diet would not seem too odd or strange to us today — people ate deer, fish, waterfowl, turtle and shellfish, nuts, berries, and wild plants.

There are several Archaic sites included in parks you can visit. There is not necessarily a lot you can learn about Archaic lifestyles by visiting these parks, since none has special exhibits, but you can get an idea of the kinds of places Archaic people lived. Raddatz Rock Shelter is in the Natural Bridge State Park in Sauk County. This site is very important for Wisconsin prehistory because it provided evidence for a sequence of cultures living in a natural rockshelter, protected from the elements. The excavations provided context and dates for some of the important diagnostic artifacts of the Archaic period. Two Late Archaic, or so-called Old Copper, sites can also be visited, although again, there are no formal exhibits about the Late Archaic to see at these parks. Old Copper State Park is at Oconto, and the Osceola site is now part of the Grant River Recreation Area in Grant County, near Potosi.

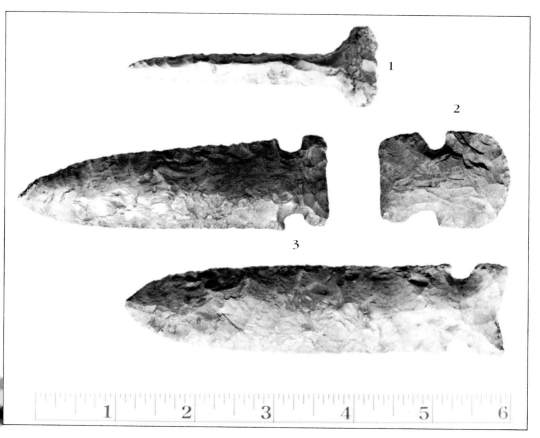

Implements from the Osceola site in Grant County: (1) drill (2) projectile point re-worked into a scraper (3) projectile points.

Pots showing conoidal base and cord-marked and impressed body.

The Woodland People:
The First Potters and Gardeners in Wisconsin

The Beginnings and Background of the Woodland Period

The Woodland period began about 1000 B.C., and like the Archaic, is divided by archaeologists into *Early Woodland* (1000-300 B.C.), *Middle Woodland* 300 B.C.-A.D. 400), and *Late Woodland* (A.D. 400-1100). Each of these different periods will be discussed after a general review of Woodland adaptations.

The Woodland period was always noted for the introduction of pottery, burial mounds, and cultivated plants. As we have just learned, however, burial mounds may have had their real forerunner in the Late Archaic cultures, and plants had already become important during the Archaic, even if people were not technically cultivating them. The only distinction that remains unique for Woodland is the introduction of pottery. The reason this distinction has remained so consistent is that it is part of the definition of Woodland — any time anyone finds pottery, it is automatically a Woodland (or more recent period) site. The lines drawn between different time periods or cultures are arbitrary and are often more of a covenience for the archaeologist than for anyone else. Throughout the Archaic and Woodland periods, we see increasing complexity and changing adaptations, but all are based on what came before. It is difficult, for example, to really tell the difference between Late Archaic and Early Woodland — the only difference is whether or not pottery is found. The different time periods and cultures discussed in this book are useful nonetheless, because they allow us to describe and explain the changes which took place in prehistory. It is probably helpful, however, if you remember that there are not clear dividing lines between these periods.

As in the preceding Late Archaic period, Woodland people hunted and fished, but plant foods became more and more important. Plants, especially nuts and seeds, were a reliable source of food, and could be easily renewed by accidental and/or purposeful planting. People were already used to collecting, processing, and eating plant remains, so the next step, planting and agriculture, which came at the end of the Woodland period, was not really such a big jump.

Pottery is one of the most important kinds of artifacts to an archaeologist. Different pottery shapes can tell us something about functions or uses of vessels. The temper, style, and thickness may indicate age, and the decoration and surface treatment may tell something about the people who made the pot and their social groups. Archaeologists study the design types and design sequences on pottery to examine the similarity between different areas and the possible closeness of relationship between different groups. Pottery styles allow archaeologists to determine age more reliably and precisely as well, since pottery styles often are started by one person or group, become very common or popular for a while, then die out and become replaced by another style.

Early Woodland people, Wisconsin's first potters, probably copied their designs and shapes from the basket, gourd, or leather containers they were already using, or possibly from the shape of their pits dug into the ground for cooking and storage. Early Woodland pottery is often thick, straight-walled, and flat-bottomed or conoidally shaped (pointed bottom). The pots were probably made by coiling and/or paddling. To coil a pot, the potter rolls the clay into a long "rope" or coil, and gradually builds the pot by curling the coil around and adding more coils. The coiled layer is pinched to attach it to the previous coil, then the coils are thinned. Thinning is done by squeezing and smoothing with the fingers and hand, by using a wooden paddle, or in later periods, by using a pottery trowel. To make a pot by paddling, the potter takes a lump of clay and pounds it into shape by holding the clay against a stone or anvil set-up of some sort, then paddling the clay with a wooden paddle. The paddles were often covered with woven fabric or cords, and the fabric or cord marking became impressed on the wet clay vessel walls. This type of surface treatment is called cordmarking and it is distinctive of Woodland cultures. No prehistoric people in Wisconsin used the potter's wheel.

Clay by itself will crack when drying and will not make a good pot when fired — it will not hold up to water, heat and regular use. To make a pot which is sturdy and useful, the potter adds something to the clay. Temper is the hard or aplastic material added to the wet clay to make it appropriate for pottery. During the Early Woodland period, small chunks of crushed stone (called grit) were used as tempering material. Later, people discovered how to grind the stone more finely, and the pottery became thinner and smoother. During Middle Woodland times, crushed limestone, sand, and grit were used, and Late Woodland people generally also used finely crushed grit.

Some prehistoric potters used grog tempering (crushed pottery). A distinctive characteristic of the Mississippian period discussed in the next chapter is its shell-tempered pottery Archaeologists sometimes use the tempering, thickness, and overall style of manufacture to determine the relative age of a piece of pottery.

The Early Woodland period (1000-300 B.C.) is noted for the introduction of pottery, but the adaptation seems to be a continuation of the basic Late Archaic lifestyle. The distinction between Early Woodland and Late Archaic is unclear unless you happen to find pottery. Early Woodland pottery, called Marion Thick in Wisconsin, is thick, somewhat crudely made, and is usually grit-tempered and cordmarked. A better-made and thinner Early Woodland pottery style which is probably later in time is called Dane Incised. Dane Incised pottery has incised lines or dashes over the cordmarking; these lines were incised into the pottery before it was fired.

Hopewell and the
Middle Woodland Period

During the Middle Woodland period (300 B.C.-A.D. 400), a series of local cultures participated in a wide range of subsistence and settlement practices. These practices followed the patterns established by earlier groups, modified by local developments and interactions. While there are some similarities between the different groups, they appear to represent somewhat different cultures and adaptations.

In Wisconsin, there were apparently two major adaptations during the Middle Woodland period. In northern Wisconsin, lakeside villages become

Woodland house, Chippewa Indians.

Some common Wisconsin Woodland projectile points.

Cylindrical copper beads used ornamentally, Trempealeau County.

Ungrooved copper axe and copper ear spools.

Chalcedony blade from Nicholls Mound, top; chalcendony knives, below and right.

Nicholls Mound, Trempeleau County.

popular and common. These villages are probably the result of greater reliance on spring and summer fishing, and are probably correlated with the use of fish nets. Winter hunting for moose, bear, woodland caribou, beaver, and hare was still very important. This northern Wisconsin tradition is generally known to archaeologists as the Laurel tradition.

In southern Wisconsin, subsistence during the Middle Woodland period begins to change. Early in the period, hunting, fishing, and collecting (especially plant seeds) were important. The location of sites in riverine settings, the relatively large site size with deep village deposits, and the kinds and quantities of other resources being used, suggest that seeds had become a major subsistence focus. Many archaeologists have suggested that horticulture or gardening (not farming) was practiced during the Middle Woodland period. Regardless of how the seeds were obtained, the presence of an abundant and storable food resource added a margin of reliability.

The Middle Woodland period is the time of an elaborate phenomenon called Hopewell. That phenomenon, which archaeologists used to think was a separate culture, was dynamic and impressive, leaving earthworks on a large scale, and imaginative art work in copper, mica, stone and other materials as the most visible evidence of its existence. Trade networks existed earlier in the region, but on nowhere near the same scale. Hopewell is known from Kansas City to New York, and from Florida to the Great Lakes; some of the exotic items which were traded include copper from the Lake Superior region, shells from the Gulf coast, and obsidian from Yellowstone National Park. People still had their local ways of doing everyday things, but Hopewell was a broad-scale phenomenon which overlaid these regional traditions. While Hopewell was not a separate culture, it is not necessarily clear what it represented. The closest term that archaeologists have come to accept is "interaction sphere." Highly prized materials came from great distances and were exchanged. But, relatively few people had access to these things. It is the first evidence of what can be considered wealth and power, with distinct ranking of people in a group.

There were two major centers of Hopewell development. One was in Ohio, the other in the central and lower Illinois River Valley. The Illinois branch of the Hopewell Interaction Sphere is known as Havana Hopewell, and Havana is the tradition which also influenced and interacted with many of the Middle Woodland populations of Wisconsin. Of the two major Hopewell branches, Illinois is less spectacular than Ohio, although both represent complex and impressive cultural systems. Both the plainer, presumably utilitarian, Havana pottery, and the more elaborate and finely made Hopewell pottery occur in Wisconsin Middle Woodland sites. Burial in Middle Woodland societies was primarily in mounds, and these mounds sometimes have central tombs for individuals of apparently higher social status who are the recipients of the elaborate Hopewell goods. While most Middle Woodland burials are placed in mounds, not all burials qualified for placement in the central tomb.

In Wisconsin Hopewell sites, archaeologists have recovered finely detailed, chipped stone ceremonial blades made of chalcedony from North Dakota, Ohio jasper, and obsidian from Yellowstone. Ground stone artifacts include platform pipes (elbow pipes are characteristic of Late Woodland, and tubular pipes are characteristic of Early Woodland) and gorgets. The Middle Woodland people of Wisconsin are the only prehistoric group who used silver — they made beads by covering a wooden core with a thin sheet of Lake Superior silver. Copper was hammered into sheets and was used to make a variety of ornaments — beads, pendants, head and breast plates, and earspools. Copper was also used to make celts (a type of ungrooved axe), awls, and panpipes (a musical instrument). A bit of textile stuck to a copper breast plate at one site in southwestern Wisconsin indicates that these people knew weaving and wore cloth garments. They apparently also wore freshwater pearls and bear canine teeth.

Middle Woodland in southern Wisconsin has strong ties to the Havana tradition; Middle Woodland in northern Wisconsin is called Laurel, and while they built mounds and made pottery with some similarities to Hopewell, it is a different regional tradition which apparently lasts longer than Middle Woodland in the southern part of the state. The greatest concentration of Middle Woodland sites, especially with Hopewell ties, is in southwestern Wisconsin, along the Mississippi River. Given the importance of trade to the Hopewell system, this placement is hardly surprising.

Economic, political, and religious or ceremonial dimensions are all a part of Hopewell. Greater dependence on plant foods meant food supplies were

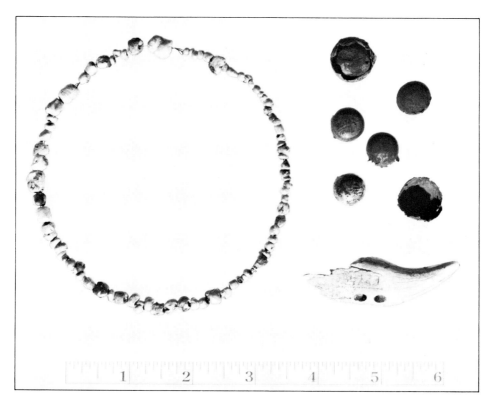

Freshwater pearls from Nicholls Mound, silver beads made of a wood core covered with a thin sheet of silver, and a bear tooth ornament.

Platform pipe characteristic of Middle Woodland Period.

49

Copper breast plate with fragments of nettle-fiber textile.

Pot showing design areas outlined by incised lines.

Quartzite blades.

relatively stable compared to dependence on hunting of animals, and it is clear that these people built on the earlier trade networks of the Late Archaic people. But the differences are major — people were treated differentially, ceremonialism abounds, and the most important in the society were treated to elaborate ceremonies, tombs and mounds, and exotic grave goods at their deaths.

Curiously, there is little evidence of conflict. In a ranked society, one might expect conflict, since it produces a collected wealth that is usually inherited. But Hopewell was different — it was not really ranked in the way we think of status and rank today. Among the Hopewell, wealth was taken out of circulation and placed with the dead; the items may have symbolized office or position or group membership more than the individual. In 1953, this book presented Hopewell as a culture separate from Woodland societies. We now know that this is not true and that Hopewell is not in itself a culture. Unfortunately, there is still a lot to learn about Hopewell and Middle Woodland, and we must learn to look past the fancy artifacts to the organizations of the various participating societies. Hopewell may have represented an elaborate way of ensuring that food and other resources were distributed over the landscape. The trade networks which existed before Middle Woodland times probably operated for the same reason, and the Hopewell system might be the ultimate elaboration on this scheme, with the elaboration serving to justify its existence across such a huge area and for so many people.

One Middle Woodland Hopewell site in Wisconsin which you can visit is referred to as Trempealeau, located in Perrot State Park in Trempealeau County. The Trempealeau site is one of the most famous Middle Woodland Hopewell sites in Wisconsin, and it is considered an important link in the Hopewell Interaction Sphere. Although there are not interpretive exhibits at the park, you can see the Middle Woodland mounds.

Around A.D. 400, Hopewell ceased to exist. The societies which immediately followed did not have artifacts and ceremonial practices which were as elaborate as Hopewell, and many people have argued that there was a cultural decline. While it is true that the pottery and other artifacts of the succeeding Late Woodland period are plainer, the culture did not decline or become less *organizationally* complex. In fact, Late Woodland was the time of beginning development toward agriculture, increased populations, more settled village life, and introduction of the bow and arrow. Rather than a decline, the Late Woodland period perhaps more accurately reflects a shift in orientation from a widespread interaction network to an intensive, localized development. Our interpretation of a decline is *ethnocentric;* that is, we are placing our own value judgments on another culture, rather than evaluating that culture on its own terms. Quite simply, we're so impressed with Hopewell artifacts, we can only interpret their disappearance as a cultural decline. We will exmaine this "decline" in more detail in the next section.

Effigy mound shapes

(a) concial

(b) linear

(c) panther

(d) eagle

(e) water fowl

(f) bird

(g) bear

(h) buffalo

(i) turtle

(j) lizard

A

B

C

F

E

D

G

H

I

J

Turtle effigy mound, Lake Koshkonong.

Late Woodland and Effigy Mound Groups

During the period from A.D. 400-1634, there were several periods of climatic fluctuation. These fluctuations did not have any dramatic effect on the plants and animals of Wisconsin, but from time to time they influenced the type and distribution of environments, and thus the adaptations of cultures which practiced horticulture or gardening.

During the Late Woodland period, the people in the southern Great Lakes region were within the limits of reliable agriculture, and over time, these societies probably became more dependent upon cultivated plant foods. There is clear evidence of the gradual development of larger and more stable residential units, but no clear indication for Late Woodland agriculture. The importance of plant foods to Late Woodland peoples has been interpreted as implying horticulture or gardening. It certainly implies intensive and systematic collecting of plant foods. Seasonal hunts, devoted almost exclusively to deer, elk or bison, were also important to economic security. Hunting or fishing may have taken place during a period when they would not interfere with agricultural or gathering activities — e.g., during early summer and especially late winter. From detailed archaeological surveys of entire regions and excavations of various site types, from analysis of the natural history of game animals, and by comparison with the practices of modern groups, it is likely that some hunts were undertaken at some distance from the village, and might last for several months.

As discussed above, for many years archaeologists have discussed a "cultural decline" after Hopewell, and a resurgence during the subsequent Mississippian period. Late Woodland has been treated as something of a cultural backwater. This perspective has been challenged in recent years and the situation deserves closer attention.

Hopewell represents elaborate burial mounds, exotic trade items, fancy symbolic goods, and large earthworks. Late Woodland societies still had burial mounds, and in Wisconsin there are effigy mounds, but the degree of elaboration was less — pottery was relatively plain, exotic materials were less frequent, and the trade networks do not seem to be operating, at least not to the same extent. People concluded that Hopewell fell apart and people reverted to simpler ways of life.

Recently, archaeologists have begun to see that the traditional perspective of a Hopewell decline only looks at artifacts, and does not examine the organization of the society. As a simplified example, look at the trappings of the Victorian period in the United States. There were elaborate houses with gargoyles, curlicues, and columns; fancy dress; lots of statues and elaborate public buildings. These things are impressive even today. After that time, however, things were not as elaborate. Did our society decline? No; our priorities changed and other things became more important. An analogous, but more substantive, situation may have been operating during the Woodland period, but one must look beyond the artifacts to examine the situation.

During the Middle Woodland period,

people began to focus on plant foods and began to develop a stable, storable resource base. This developed further in the Late Woodland period to an eventual dependence on agriculture, but a clear orientation to plant resources before that. The shift toward food production takes time and energy, with concentration on the local habitat. Late Woodland people may have turned their attention toward this adaptation, forcing a reordering of priorities to their immediate environment. As this way of life grew and developed, larger and more stable communities were established, and eventually culminated in the Mississippian period, the most complex of prehistoric cultures in the eastern United States. The Mississippian culture is built on an agricultural base, with trade, division of labor, and a complex social organization. Aztalan in Jefferson County, Wisconsin, is an example of a Mississippian site, and will be discussed in the next chapter.

If Late Woodland is examined from the perspective of organization, no decline is apparent. Instead, one sees larger populations, larger and more stable villages, more substantial houses, an emphasis on food storage, development of the bow and arrow, and strong community development. Artifacts alone clearly do not reveal the entire picture.

During the Late Woodland period, there were three varieties of adaptations in Wisconsin — fishermen and hunters of the northern forests who practiced no agriculture or horticulture; people of the transitional zone between the northern conifer and southern deciduous forests who practiced horticulture to varying degrees, but who could not regularly depend upon cultivated plants; and finally, the societies in the southern part of the region who could rely on cultivation to a greater extent.

The northern hunters and fishermen did well because of the abundant fish resources of the Great Lakes and the numerous inland lakes and waterways. The population density and summer residential stability was high — the pattern was broken only during late winter when limited food resources necessitated a temporary reversion to a smaller family-band hunting economy.

In the transition zone, there are economies which were oriented toward the collection and use of food plants. The amount of food produced depended upon the geographic position, climatic episodes, and yearly fluctuations in the length of the growing season. For example, during the period from A.D. 800-1200, there were people practicing effective corn agriculture farther north than in preceding or subsequent periods. Nonetheless, neither plant collecting nor horticulture was reliable enough to warrant exclusive effort. Hunting, gathering, and particularly fishing, were important.

In southern Wisconsin, people focused on cultivated plants to a greater extent, but also heavily utilized other resources which were available in varying quantities in different microenvironments. This was a period of territorialization, with different groups laying claim to specific areas.

While some archaeologists think that agriculture became important in southern Wisconsin during the Late Woodland period, there is no detailed evidence to support this theory. It is

An "elbow" pottery pipe, characteristic of the Late Woodland period. Contrast this with the Middle Woodland platform pipe.

likely, however, that Late Woodland societies were territorial and were oriented to collecting and using large quantities of plant foods. In southern Wisconsin, recent work has suggested that the natural resources of the rich wetland areas may have been more important, more immediately available, and more desirable than agriculture to the Late Woodland people. In any event, the Late Woodland period represents a change or reorientation of groups to the immediate land and territory.

While not as elaborate as Hopewell mounds, there are unusual mound types which were built during the Late Woodland period, and Wisconsin is the major location for these unique kinds of mounds. The mounds are called "effigy mounds" and are so-named because they were built in the shape of various birds and other animals. The Effigy Mound tradition refers to the Late Woodland cultures who built

these mounds. The most common effigy mound shapes are referred to as panther, turtle, bird, and bear. The mounds usually average about three feet in height, and in addition to mounds in the shapes of animals, the mound groups usually include small conical mounds and elongated linear mounds. Some of the mounds may have a burial or two in them, but many of the mounds are empty, with no burials or artifacts. Most archaeologists place the Effigy Mound tradition in the Late Woodland period, but some have argued that Effigy Mound begins before Late Woodland (at about A.D. 300) and continues after Late Woodland (until as late as A.D. 1642). Whatever the case, Effigy Mound seems to represent an indigenous development, based on a hunting, fishing, and collecting economy, although some archaeologists have suggested that these people may also have practiced farming, or at least gardening.

Although Effigy Mounds are concentrated in Wisconsin, primarily in the southern half of the state, such mounds are also found in adjacent portions of Minnesota, Iowa, and Illinois. The Effigy Mound tradition has been defined by the presence of the mounds themselves and Madison ware ceramics. Unfortunately, Madison ceramics are a broad category and are so widespread and variable in type and distribution, the definition becomes similar to saying the mounds are Woodland. There are regional differences within and between Effigy Mound clusters, and archaeologists are trying to discover ways to examine these differences and their meaning.

The current interpretation of the Effigy Mounds ties them to territorial boundaries. Given our knowledge of Late Woodland cultures, this does not seem unreasonable. The general interpretation is that the mound groups probably represent clans or some other territorial group. The mounds may be territory markers, or they may be yearly or semi-yearly gathering places for the clans or groups. Late Woodland people, whether agricultural or not, tended to be semi-nomadic — they moved once or twice a year to most effectively exploit their environment. While villages with plant resources and other items could feed people during the summer and early fall, it was difficult to feed large numbers of people during the winter, when food was in short supply. Groups would regularly disperse into smaller units during the winter, then aggregate into the larger group during the spring, thereby taking best advantage of the available resources. Effigy Mounds tend to be located near lakes and rivers with extensive wetlands; this location is ideal since it is next to rich resources for seasonal gathering and dispersal activities. It is possible that Effigy Mound burials simply represent those individuals who died while their group was dispersed, or who died just before dispersal.

One of the most unusual types of Effigy Mounds is not a mound at all. It is a form called an "intaglio," and it is actually a "negative" mound, formed by scooping out the earth to leave an indented impression of an animal. Intaglios are shallow, maybe a foot deep, and contain no burials. Less than a dozen intaglios have ever been reported, and all are either panther or bear in shape. The only complete surviving intaglio is in Fort Atkinson in Jefferson County. The panther intaglio is along the Rock River, on the north side of State Highway 106, just west of downtown Fort Atkinson; a historic marker indicates the location.

Of all the various types of archaeological sites in Wisconsin, Effigy Mound sites are the easiest to visit, since so many of them have been made into parks. The following is a list of the Effigy Mound sites which are open to the public. Lizard Mounds State Park in Washington County (near West Bend), and the Effigy Mounds National Monument across the Mississippi River in McGregor, Iowa, are especially worth a visit. In both cases, exhibits and interpretive signs will help you to better understand the site.

Site name/Park name	County/Town/State
Lizard Mounds State Park	*Washington/West Bend, WI*
Kleizten Mounds (Sheboygan Indian Mound Park)	*Sheboygan, WI*
High Cliff State Park	*Sherwood, WI*
Beloit College Mounds (on the campus)	*Beloit, WI*
Kegonza State Park	*Kegonza, WI*
Arboretum Mounds	*Madison (UW-Madison), WI*
Devil's Lake State Park	*Baraboo, WI*
Nelson Dewey State Park	*Cassville, WI*
Weyalusing State Park	*Prairie du Chien, WI*
Effigy Mound National Monument	*McGregor, IA*

Clam Lake mound, Burnett County.

The Mississippian People of Wisconsin: Farmers and Traders

The Mississippian period (A.D. 1000-1500) can be divided into Middle Mississippian and Upper Mississippian. The distinction is largely one of geography and subsequent differences in adaptation, although Upper Mississippian is thought to have continued into more recent times.

Middle Mississippian Adaptations — Aztalan and Points South

Middle Mississippian is characterized by permanent stockaded villages; pyramidal mounds; plaza areas; well-made shell-tempered pottery with incised and engraved designs; a great variety of vessel shapes, including plates, beakers, bottles, bowls, and jars; maize, beans, and squash agriculture; and social stratification. Middle Mississippian society was hierarchically organized with large towns surrounded by smaller villages, hamlets, farmsteads, and camps. Aztalan, in Jefferson County between Milwaukee and Madison, is believed by many to be a northern outpost of Middle Mississippian society.

While development of Middle Mississippian society was thought to have taken place at the Cahokia site, in East St. Louis, Illinois, it is not clear whether Aztalan is directly related to the people at Cahokia, or indirectly related through Middle Mississippian groups who occupied portions of northern Illinois. A few other sites believed to be Middle Mississippian have been discovered in Wisconsin in recent years, but Aztalan remains the clearest, largest, and best-known example of the Middle Mississippian presence in Wisconsin.

A reconstruction of how Aztalan might have looked is presented in a drawing. The village encompassed a twenty-one acre area, and was surrounded by a palisade, plastered with clay and equipped with bastions or "watchtowers" at intervals of about eighty feet. There are remains of three stockades, suggesting that several had been destroyed, or fell into disrepair and were rebuilt. Parts of the stockade wall have been reconstructed at the site, and one can get an impression of how the stockade may have looked.

Within the village were three mounds: one in the northwest corner, one in the southwest corner, and a third (which is no longer visible) in the northeast part of the site. All three mounds were flat-topped or pyramidal in shape, and were built in three stages. Each mound held some sort of ceremonial structure on top, and none of the three was specifically used for burial.

Within the stockaded area were sectioned areas with the remains of houses. The people at Aztalan built their houses in a variety of styles, usually in either a circular or rectangular pattern. The houses had pole supports with wattle-and-daub plaster (a mixture of grasses or fibers with clay) and thatched roofs. When burned, the wattle-and-daub mixture becomes fired almost like pottery, and this has been called "Aztalan brick." The people at Aztalan grew corn, but they also used many of the plants which grow wild in the region, such as hickory nuts and acorns, and a variety of berries and other plant foods. They ate a lot of deer meat, but evidence of elk, raccoon, beaver, muskrat, and fox has also been found. Fish was another favorite food, and the Aztalan people ate catfish, bass, suckers, buffalofish, pike, drum, and gar. Mussels (freshwater clams) were frequently part of the diet, as well as

Dish with raised sides, left; beaker, right rear, gourd-shaped ladle, front.

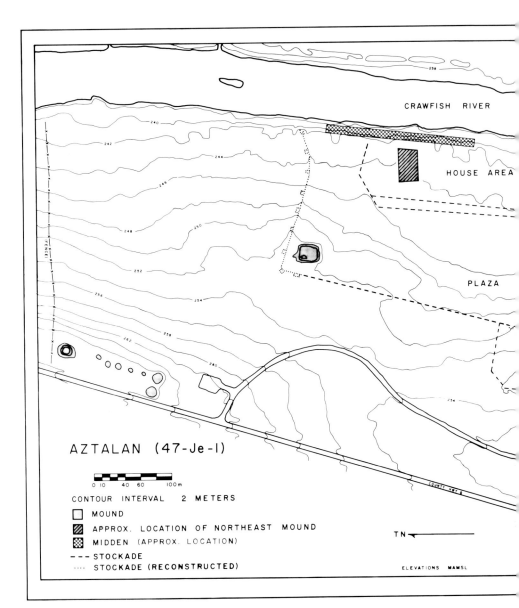

CRAWFISH RIVER

HOUSE AREA

PLAZA

AZTALAN (47-Je-I)

0 10   40 60   100m

CONTOUR INTERVAL   2 METERS

☐ MOUND
▨ APPROX. LOCATION OF NORTHEAST MOUND
▧ MIDDEN (APPROX. LOCATION)
- - - STOCKADE
···· STOCKADE (RECONSTRUCTED)

TN ◄

ELEVATIONS MAMSL

Map of Aztalan, Jefferson County.

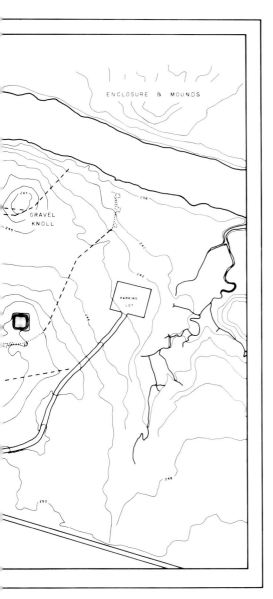

ENCLOSURE & MOUNDS

GRAVEL
KNOLL

PARKING
LOT

turtles and a variety of birds such as passenger pigeons, ducks, teals, turkeys, geese and swans. The only animal domesticated by these people was the dog; some dog burials have been found at the site.

People need resources other than clay and stone for building houses and making other kinds of tools. Turtle shells were often made into bowls; mussel shells were used to make spoons and beads and other jewelry; wood was used for building houses, making arrow shafts and bowls; and various bones were used to make awls, points, and pins. The fur from animals makes excellent clothing and blankets, and branches and grasses were used to make thatch and bedding. Some items were used immediately, others were processed and stored for later use. Some raw materials were locally available, other items were imported from great distances.

There are two popular notions about Aztalan which archaeologists would like to dispel. The first is that the site is related to the Aztecs of Mexico. There is no evidence for this at all. Although some relationship to Cahokia is present, there is absolutely nothing about Aztalan which links it to the Aztecs. This myth began when Nathaniel Hyer, who first described the site, indicated he thought the place might be the northern site referred to in Aztec legend. Because of his idea, he called the site Aztalan. However, other than the name given to the site by Hyer, there is no evidence for either an Aztec or Mexican connection.

The second notion about Aztalan which must be discussed is the presumed cannibalism. The only evidence for cannibalism at Aztalan is that some

Mussel shell hoe with a hole for a handle attachment, and beads cut from mussel shells.

Chipped stone hoe.

broken human bones were found in garbage and refuse pits within the site. There is a great deal of misunderstanding and oversimplification about what these bones might mean. First, we know that no human society ever ate human flesh for nutritional reasons on a regular basis. All known cases of frequent or usual cannibalism are what is called "ritual cannibalism." This means that the flesh of a dead person was eaten (but only one or two bites or by means of a gesture) to acquire one or more of the dead person's characteristics, or to protect the living from the ghost of the dead. One common example is when a warrior died or was killed in combat; people in some societies would eat a taste of the person to gain the strengths, skills, or other qualities of the dead warrior. Second, many societies "process" the bodies of their dead. In some cultures, some parts of the body have greater importance than others. Thus, some parts may be curated or kept for years before burial, while other parts are discarded — literally thrown in the garbage. Sometimes people are buried immediately, other times they are not. There is great variability in the treatment of the dead across the world. "Processing," or different stages of treatment of the dead, is a common practice, and is well documented for both Late Woodland and Mississippian societies. This practice is often an act of respect, and can indicate that the person was important within the society. There is no clear evidence of cannibalism at Aztalan — what is clear is that the people of Aztalan had ways of treating their dead which differ from ours.

We do not know what happened to the people who lived at Aztalan. It is not clear whether they moved away, were forced out, were burned out, or what. There is no known surviving historic Indian group which is clearly related, and the answers to the mysteries of the site may be addressed by further investigations, but will probably still be around for future generations of archaeologists to solve.

Aztalan today is a state park, but because of budgetary problems, it is currently being managed by the Township of Aztalan. If you visit Aztalan during the summer or fall, you can walk around the site and see a small interpretive display.

Upper Mississippian Adaptations — Oneota Cultures

Upper Mississippian, called Oneota in Wisconsin, is thought to be related to Middle Mississippian society and perhaps derived from it, although there is also some evidence for a partial continuation of a local Late Woodland adaptation. While there is some evidence for maize agriculture in Oneota societies, hunting, fishing, and collecting of other plants were still of major importance. Some archaeologists claim that Oneota is simply the Middle Mississippian adaptation to a more northerly climate.

Characteristics of Oneota societies include permanent villages in lake and riverine areas; triangular projectile points; shell-tempered ceramics with plain surfaces, broad trailing and flared rims; and burial in low mounds or cemeteries. Other chipped stone tools include drills, scrapers, and "four-edged" or willow-shaped knives. Ground stone tools include celts, adzes, discoidals used in a type of game, and

Mortar on which corn was ground with a muller or grinding stone, left; ungrooved axe or celt, right.

Discoidal, believed to have been used in a game in which it served as a rolling target for a spear, left; copper ear spool, right.

Pot showing characteristic Oneota globular shape.

several kinds of pipes. Bone and shell were used to make awls, fishhooks, fish lures, musical instruments, pendants, beads and bracelets. Metal working was limited to tubular copper beads and pendants cut out of sheet copper. Oneota overlaps with Middle Mississippian and may continue into the historic period in some localities.

Although Oneota artifacts can be found in many areas of the state, Oneota settlements tend to be clustered in the southern half of the state along some of the major waterways and lake shores. In particular, it appears that Oneota settlements are often found near large lakes and associated wetlands along major river systems. Probably as many as 70-90 people lived in some of the larger Oneota villages, with maize and other food stored in deep pits for later use. The association of Oneota settlements with wetlands may have to do with creating a better atmosphere for agriculture — recent excavations near LaCrosse suggest that garden beds or corn fields were placed in wetland settings to take advantage of the richest soils and the generally warmer temperatures in wetlands.

Like the Middle Mississippian people at Aztalan, we don't know what happened to the Oneota people. Some archaeologists have argued that at least some Oneota groups became the present-day Winnebago and Ioway Indians. If true, there is no clear evidence for this association from any archaeological site or excavation; these theories remain unconfirmed. As with all areas of Wisconsin prehistory, we have a made a good start, and we have cleared up some problems, but there are many questions left to answer.

Mussel shell spoon, top; shell pendant, far left, pendants cut from copper.

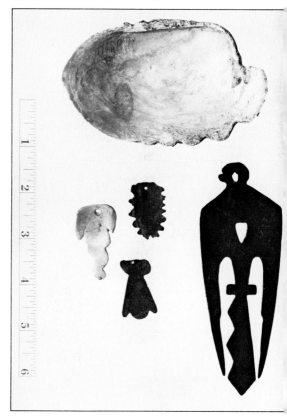

Bone-splint awl, top; incised bone bead, left; bone fish hook, center, shell fish lure, right. A line was attached to upper hole to attract fish within spearing range.

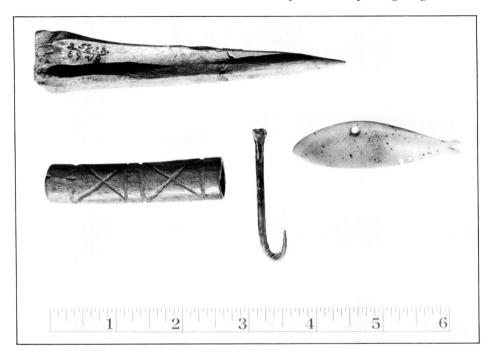

Willow leaf knive, top; end scraper, left, triangular arrowhead, right.

Plan view of buried Oneota ridged fields near LaCrosse. The alternating light and dark bands represent the ridges and furrows.

This view provides another perspective of the ridged field cross-section. Notice how much soil has washed in since the ridges were in use. Scale is in inches.

A close-up view of one of the ridges. Several stages of construction are visible. The first stage is represented by the dark ridges, then lighter fill washed in; this layer was then capped by another stage of ridge construction.

Making plaster casts of bird petroglyphs at Twin Bluffs, Juneau County.

Wisconsin Prehistory
Today and Tomorrow

What Is Left to be Learned &
How Can You Help?

While we have learned a considerable amount about Wisconsin's prehistory since 1953, there is still much to be learned. Some mysteries will be resolved by future generations, and some will, perhaps, never be fully explained.

What exactly happened at the end of the Middle Woodland and Mississippian periods, and how did it happen? Why did some groups build effigy mounds, why did others never build them, and why did people stop building mounds? What is the significance of the various pictures and drawings carved into rocks and cliffs and caves throughout Wisconsin? Why did prehistoric trade develop at certain points in prehistory, and then become seemingly unimportant at others?

The present citizens of Wisconsin should be aware of the rich heritage to be found here. We need not look with envy at other areas or other countries. Mounds, garden beds, village sites, and petroglyphs should be regarded as valuable resources of our community. Every effort must be made to preserve these resources for the wonder and enlightenment of coming generations. No mound or site should be excavated except by qualified, authorized archaeologists; once the untrained shovel disturbs a site, much of the information that lies within is destroyed forever. Discoveries of artifacts or burials should be reported to archaeologists at museums or universities — such discoveries might be important and may contribute to our knowledge of the early inhabitants of the state.

Amateur archaeologists, farmers, and others who happen to find artifacts are sometimes our only clue to archaeological sites which have since been destroyed by urban expansion. People have collected some sites for many years, and have a far broader and larger collection of materials from the sites than archaeologists could ever hope to gather. The willingness of the public to share knowledge has helped many archaeologists to better understand the regions in which they work.

Unfortunately, not all collectors are helpful — many seriously damage or even destroy our archaeological resources. Some are a threat to our understanding of the past. What is the difference between good and bad? A few simple practices make all the difference in the world:

1. If you find an artifact or group of artifacts, be sure to note exactly where you found it and when. Catalogue your finds — if nothing else, keep things that were found very close to each other together. Keep the items separated from those found elsewhere.

2. Contact an archaeologist about your finds. Most colleges and universities in Wisconsin have archaeologists who would be happy to record the information about your finds. If you are uncertain about whom to call, contact the State Historical Society in Madison. Be ready and willing to tell the archaeologist all you can about your site or sites. The archaeologist will not "steal" your site or broadcast its location — you will be helping to piece together essential knowledge of the past, and you may learn how old your artifacts are, as well as something about the people who made the artifacts.

3. Most importantly, do not buy, sell, or trade artifacts of known location. Once this happens, the most important information — the context — is gone forever.

4. Never excavate a site without proper supervision because once a site is excavated it is gone and can never be reconstructed.

You can help archaeologists a great deal, but only if you treat each archaeological site and artifact as a finite resource that can never be replaced once it has been destroyed. The future of the past is up to us.

Protecting the Past —
Laws and Archeology

Although there are many archaeological sites all over the world, they nevertheless represent a non-renewable resource, and once a site is destroyed it is gone forever. For decades, archaeologists and private citizens clamored about the importance of protecting archaeological sites, but it was not until the 1960s that some progress was made in the United States. Laws were drafted to help protect the natural and cultural resources of the nation, a long extablished tradition in many European countries.

The federal laws which deal with antiquities have created a policy of managing or conserving archaeological resources — not just salvaging something before the bulldozer enters. There are some who get very upset by the idea that their tax dollars are spent on archaeology, yet the proportionate amount of money spent is very small, and the return very great.

One set of laws (National Environmental Policy Act of 1969, National

Historic Preservation Act, and Executive Order 11593) provides guidelines on how to assess the impact of proposed construction on archaeological sites. These acts define a philosophy of government decision making, requiring that environmental and cultural variables be considered side by side with technological and economic benefits when planning construction. Archaeological reports which result from these studies detail the nature of the archaeological resources endangered, and how the impact of the projects should be altered, either by changing the proposed construction or by excavation of the sites.

Another important piece of legislation is the Archaeological and Historic Preservation Act of 1974. This act requires federal agencies to consider the dangers to archaeological sites posed by their activities. These agencies are authorized to spend up to one percent of their project money for archaeological work before any of their construction activities begin.

Some of you may have heard of the National Register of Historic Places. The creation of this register was mandated by the National Historic Preservation Act of 1966, and provides a way for significant archaeological, historical, and architectural resources to be recognized. If an archaeologist or any other citizen thinks that an archaeological site is especially well-preserved or important, he or she can fill out a description of the site on a set of special forms, and nominate the site or area to the National Register. This nomination first goes to a state-wide Historic Preservation Review Board appointed by the Governor. If the state board agrees that the site is significant,

Petroglyphs in Dodge County. The carvings were made in slate between sections of quartzite bedrock.

they forward the nomination to Washington where a national review board examines the nomination. If the national board thinks the nomination is worthy, they will place the site on the National Register of Historic Places.

What does listing on the National Register of Historic Places mean? The major benefits or implications can be summarized as follows: 1) it is a note of distinction for the site, and indicates its special significance for our cultural heritage; 2) if a project involving federal funds or federal permits will endanger the site, the danger to the site must be taken into consideration, either by excavation of the site or by change of the project plans; 3) if a site is already on the National Register and a project involving federal money or federal permits is planned, time and money can be saved since a detailed survey and nomination procedure may not be necessary; 4) for owners of National Register sites, it may be possible to get property tax breaks for perserving these sites. If you own a site which is placed on the National Register, it will not restrict your ability to do things — plans for your land can usually proceed without interference. The only time that the listing is important is if the project involves federal funds or permits, and then, having the site on the Register may be a benefit because the government will require you to check for archaeological resources and evaluate those resources for qualification for the Register. If a site on your land is already on the National Register, you can save a lot of the time and money required to evaluate the resources — a lot of the work is already done.

Archaeologists are *not* against progress. In fact, by including archaeologists at the planning level, the most efficient plans can be made — ensuring the desired result while minimizing the destruction of our past. Archaeologists need not hold up construction *if* they are included at the early stages of a project. Archaeological preservation and conservation does *not* mean giving up projects or not doing what you want to do; both can be accomplished. We must learn to see ourselves as the custodians, rather than the absolute owners, of the resources — we are obliged to pass this inheritance on to future generations.

Selected Bibliography

Barrett, S.A.
   1933   Ancient Aztalan. *Milwaukee Public Museum Bulletin* 13.
Griffin, James B.
   1983   The Midlands, in *Ancient North Americans* (Jesse Jennings, editor); pp. 243-301. W.H. Freeman & Co.
Lapham, I.A.
   1855   Antiquities of Wisconsin. *Smithsonian Contributions to Knowledge,* Volume 7, Article 4.
McKern, W.C.
   1942   The First Settlers of Wisconsin. *Wisconsin Magazine of History,* Volume 26, Number 2.
Mason, Ronald
   1981   *Great Lakes Archaeology.* Academic Press, New York.
Quimby, George
   1960   *Indian Life in the Upper Great Lakes.* University of Chicago Press.
Ritzenthaler, Robert E. (editor)
   1957   The Old Copper Culture of Wisconsin. *Wisconsin Archeologist* (n.s.), Volume 38, Number 4.
Silverberg, Robert
   1968   *Mound Builders of Ancient America.* New York Graphic Society, Ltd. Greenwich, Connecticut.

The Wisconsin Archeologist contains many articles of general interest on Wisconsin archaeology.

*The photographs in this publication are
from the collections of the Milwaukee
Public Museum. Additional photographs
were used courtesy of the sources listed
below:*
*Pages 4 top, 7, 9, 18, 19, 21 — University
of Wisconsin — Milwaukee*
Page 4 bottom — State Historical Society
*Page 67 — University of Wisconsin —
LaCrosse; Mississippi Valley Archaeological Center*